ESSENTIAL MANAGERS

Strategic Management

KEVAN WILLIAMS

D0808936

London, New York, Melbourne,
Munich, and Delhi

Senior Editor Peter Jones
US Editor Margaret Parrish
Senior Art Editor Helen Spencer
Production Editor Ben Marcus
Production Controller Hema Gohil
Executive Managing Editor Adèle Hayward
Managing Art Editor Kat Mead
Art Director Peter Luff
Publisher Stephanie Jackson

Produced for Dorling Kindersley Limited by
cobaltid

The Stables, Wood Farm, Deopham Road,
Attleborough, Norfolk NR17 1AJ
www.cobaltid.co.uk

Editors Kati Dye, Maddy King,
Marek Walisiewicz
Designers Paul Reid, Lloyd Tilbury

First American Edition, 2009

Published in the United States by DK Publishing
375 Hudson Street, New York, New York 10014

09 10 11   10 9 8 7 6 5 4 3 2 1

ND134—March 2009

Published in Great Britain by
Dorling Kindersley Limited.

A catalog record for this book is available from
the Library of Congress.

ISBN 978-0-7566-4859-6

DK books are available at special discounts
when purchased in bulk for sales promotions,
premiums, fund-raising, or educational use.
For details, contact: DK Publishing Special Markets,
375 Hudson Street, New York, New York 10014 or
SpecialSales@dk.com.

Color reproduction
by Colorscan, Singapore
Printed in China by WKT

Discover more at **www.dk.com**

Contents

CHAPTER 3
Creating a good strategy

CHAPTER 4
Implementing your strategy

Introduction

Strategy is about creating and delivering the future. It is about leading your team or your organization to a future in which you are able to compete more effectively and to achieve prosperity and sustainability. The skills of strategic management are applicable to those leading a team or planning the direction of any size of organization in all sectors—private, public, and voluntary.

Strategic Management is for those taking, or wanting to take, their first steps to developing and implementing strategic changes. It gives you the tools you need to make effective strategic decisions, by helping you analyze your organization and the world it operates in, plan your strategic approach, and implement the changes. It provides insight into how to gain a competitive advantage, which is at the heart of good strategy.

The most important aim of this book, however, is to encourage you to think strategically and develop your powers of strategic thinking so that they become second nature. Strategic management is easier than many suggest, yet not all managers take the time to master it. If you do develop the ability to think strategically and learn the skills needed for strategic management, you will make yourself a valuable asset to your organization.

Chapter 1

Understanding strategy

Strategy is about making sure that your business arrives where you want it to at a given time. As a manager, you need to know what good strategy looks like and understand how it can be used to create the future for your team or organization.

Planning for change

When you map out your business strategy you are creating a future that may be two, three, five, or more years ahead. It's not just the plan itself that has the value, but all the thinking that goes into it, the questions you ask yourself, and the answers that come forward.

Keeping moving

No organization can stand still. At the very least, the costs of running a business will increase year on year; prices of raw materials will rise, staff will expect higher wages, and rent will go up. This means that you must increase your output every year. And in time, you will inevitably reach a point where you cannot increase sales further in your current situation. At this point you will need to make a bigger change; this is the time to change your strategy. Strategies exist at many levels, from those that move the whole business forward to those that develop the individuals working within it.

Defining triggers

The need to change strategy is initiated by changes in your organization (internal triggers) or in the business environment (external triggers). External triggers include "big" events over which your organization has no control, but that can be anticipated and managed around, such as growth or decline in the economy, taxation changes, or new technology. More specific external triggers include a new competitor in your market, your main customer no longer needing your services, or even changes in road layouts that mean that customers no longer drive past your shop.

Internal reasons to change are similarly diverse—a change of location for the business meaning old activities are more difficult or new activities are possible, for example, or the loss of an experienced member of staff.

Setting off

Devising your strategy means setting the direction and scope of your organization, and planning how to meet the needs of your customers, over a period of years. It means identifying signposts that confirm you are heading in the right direction, and making good progress on the journey.

SUCCEEDING AT STRATEGY

FAST TRACK

OFF TRACK

FAST TRACK	OFF TRACK
Having a clear destination in mind	Being too busy with today to think about tomorrow
Being willing to deal with the big picture	Being too quick to say why something shouldn't happen
Knowing why you are better than your competitors	Not being able to quickly give the reasons why your business exists
Feeling "on top" of leading the business to a brighter future	Making decisions without referring to your overall strategic direction

Counting the benefits

Whether you are managing a team, a start-up business, a local government department, a large commercial organization, or a charity, having a good strategy will attract many benefits besides ensuring you're more likely to reach your goals. It also helps you to map out your future, attract funding, and establish a team of great people to work with.

Mapping your future

First, a good strategy acts as a road map. It should clearly identify where you want to be at a given point in time, say, three years. For example, one of your goals may be to increase sales by a factor of ten. Your strategy should set out how you will achieve this target. Boosting sales by this amount will clearly require actions bolder than printing a new sales leaflet.

A strategy has more than the destination in mind. It enables you to map the roads and junctions along the way, so that you can plot your way and, critically, measure your progress. Three years is too long to wait to see if you made the right decisions, and you need frequent reassurance that you are on the right road.

Attracting funding

Second, a clear strategy attracts interest and funding from third parties. This might be start-up finance for a new business, internal funding (where you have to compete with other teams for resources), or a bid for sponsorship. In every scenario, funders want to know that you are in control of the situation. They can't predict the future, so they seek reassurance from your confidence in your plan for the future. A considered strategy demonstrates that their funds will be well used and that they will receive a healthy and secure return.

Unifying the organization

Finally, a clear strategy acts as a unifying force within an organization. You may have worked in organizations where the staff focus only on their job and don't understand how it fits into wider processes and objectives (and perhaps don't even care). This results in confusion, frustration for staff and customers alike, and ultimately a short-term future for the organization.

By creating a clear strategy and sharing it with your team or organization, everyone knows where they are going; people are then far more likely to adjust their behavior to make the whole enterprise work better. A well-communicated strategy sends the message: "We're all in this together." Having a destination is very powerful in terms of human motivation because we are motivated in one of two ways: "away from pain" or "toward pleasure." The former leads to behavior that achieves a short-term result, but having moved away from pain we may end up in a place we are not so keen to be. If we move toward pleasure we will be more likely to achieve a goal that we want to sustain.

CASE STUDY

A driving force in retail

Now nearly one hundred years old, the UK supermarket group Tesco has demonstrated strong strategic thinking throughout its history. It became a leader in new formats (such as self-service supermarkets) and grew initially by opening new stores then through acquisition. Anticipating changing prosperity and tastes in the 1970s, Tesco moved away from its discount format. To achieve further growth, it had to find new customers. Strategically it aimed to achieve this in a number of ways: continuing growth in its core UK market, and providing new non-food services to UK food customers; finding new food customers in other countries by opening stores in China, Poland, and Turkey, among other countries; and following its customers into new retailing services. Underlying much of its strategy is its "core purpose"—to "create value for customers to earn their lifetime loyalty." Tesco is now the third-largest grocery retailer in the world, with group sales of £51.8 billion, and 3,728 stores worldwide in 13 countries, employing 440,000 staff.

Leading your competitors

Your business, and every team within it, must have a source of competitive advantage—an overriding reason why customers will want to do business with you rather than a competitor. Understanding, identifying, creating, and sustaining competitive advantage is at the heart of good strategy.

Gaining advantage

Without sustainable competitive advantage, your organization will always be vulnerable. Imagine you run a pizza restaurant in a small town, where you share the market with two competing pizzerias. You decide to win more business, so you differentiate yourself by offering a home-delivery service. Within a month your turnover has doubled: you have achieved competitive advantage. But seeing your success, your competitors also start to offer delivery and within another month, your sales have returned to their previous levels.

The problem is that this competitive advantage was just temporary. To be sustainable, competitive advantage needs to be difficult or impossible to copy. In this example, this could mean investing in more expensive premises—located between the

Q IN FOCUS... INDIRECT COMPETITION

Competition is not limited to organizations providing the same service or selling the same products. Much of your competition may be indirect. For example, for the strategic manager of a bowling alley, another bowling alley in town is a direct competitor. However, bowling is a form of family entertainment, so that manager also needs to consider competition from the movies and the local pizzeria. The leader of a team within an organization will be in direct competition with other teams within the organization that can provide the same service, but will face indirect competition from external companies that could also provide this service.

shopping center and the cinema, say—that a large number of people will pass by. Your rivals cannot occupy the same site, so you have a sustainable competitive advantage over them.

What are the potential sources of sustainable competitive advantage that your organization should seek to develop? Location is clearly key in the retail sector, but sources of sustainable competitive advantage can be identified in every industry:

• Size: being bigger gives you control of the market and achieves economies of scale
• Knowledge: a big-city law firm, for example, may have more knowledge than a smaller firm
• Resources: control of limited resources of any kind
• Relationships: key relationships with decision-makers cannot be easily copied by your competitors
• Brand: while it is easy to copy a product, it is difficult to copy the emotions customers feel about a particular brand—that's why organizations invest so heavily in brand identity.

TIP

NEVER STOP LOOKING

Always remember that everything and everyone is replaceable, so never stop looking at your competitive advantage.

Looking to the future

One of the most important aspects of strategic management is predicting the things that will impact you and your organization in the future. Some of these are bigger than you, and you cannot change them. Others are within your power to change. Knowing what you can change and what you need to work around will help you to use your resources efficiently.

Understanding major forces

Macroeconomic* factors are major forces that impact not just your organization, but also your competitors and your marketplace. They may impact other markets, the country, and sometimes the world economy. While you as a team or organization cannot change or control these things, you can seek to understand them and create strategies that fit in with them.

*Macroeconomic— related to the big aspects of an economy, such as inflation, economic growth, recession, and levels of employment.

Many other factors are within your sphere of influence, and when you control them, you can set the agenda. When you control enough factors in your environment, you become the market leader and set the standards for the whole industry: if, for example, you decide to reduce your prices, your competitors are forced to reduce theirs.

Large organizations can exert huge control—even dictating government policy—but even if you cannot aspire to this level of power, you should attempt to implement strategies that give you as much control as possible. The more control you have, the fewer surprises you'll encounter and the more likely you are to survive in the longer term. There are a number of sources of control you need to achieve to give you greater power within the environment in which you operate. Developing one or more of these will give you a greater ability to direct your particular market.

EXPERT POWER
At times we all need someone who can find solutions to our problems. Expertise is a source of power, especially when it is in short supply.

CONTROL OF KNOWLEDGE
Access to information and knowledge provides you with understanding and an enhanced ability to prepare. It places you ahead of your competitors—internal or external.

CONTROL OF RESOURCES
If you control who can use resources, such as staff, money, and offices, then you have power over other managers.

Sources of control

PERSONAL POWER
This derives from your personal influence—your ability to make people voluntarily do what you want. Influential people spend their time talking with others.

CONTROL OF DISTRIBUTION
If you are a good retailer and make your outlets popular with customers, suppliers want to talk to you. By controlling access to customers, you can control the manufacturers.

Shaping your strategy

Strategic management is necessary to achieve success in all types of organizations. However, the way strategy is understood and applied differs depending on the sector in which your organization operates, whether it is private, public, or voluntary.

Private sector strategy

The private sector is defined by competition. Companies continue to exist only if they provide products or services that are better than those of their competitors, so the concept of sustainable competitive advantage is usually at the heart of company strategy. Another key dimension of private sector strategy is time. Lead times* for developing new products and getting them to market are often short, and tension can exist between delivering short-term profits and planning and resourcing long-term strategy.

*__Lead time__— *the time it takes for a process to be completed, from the start of that process to its completion.*

Public sector strategy

The public sector delivers public policy and undertakes functions such as collecting taxes. It is largely immune to the forces of competition, although competition does exist internally, such as between departments seeking funding from a limited government pot. If public sector organizations spend less than they receive, the difference is known as "surplus", not "profit".

Strategy in the public sector is usually centered on delivering goals to satisfy the political process and producing conspicuous efficiency and value for money to reassure taxpayers. Political pressures commonly lead to changes in priorities to gain voter support, and to a short-term view that impacts upon longer-term strategic planning.

Voluntary sector strategy

Voluntary organizations can be considered to fall between the public and private sectors. While their objectives may be social or political, they are subject to the same competitive forces as the private sector. They must compete for funding from public or private organizations, and from individuals. Unlike the private sector, however, it is not always clear who the customers of a voluntary organization are—is it the recipients of funding, the donors, the trustees, or the volunteers who help make it run? Consequently, strategic management of voluntary sector organizations is heavily based upon satisfying all of these different groups, through careful stakeholder* management.

*Stakeholder—
anyone who has an interest in your organization and how it is run.

Voluntary sector organizations must be careful not to spend more than they receive in donations. Like public sector organizations, if a voluntary organization spends less than it receives, the difference is known as "surplus" rather than "profit", for social, political, and presentational reasons.

FEATURES OF PRIVATE, PUBLIC, AND VOLUNTARY SECTORS

	PRIVATE	PUBLIC	VOLUNTARY
Who is the customer?	Organizations in the market	The public and political leaders	Donors, recipients, and volunteers
What are the competitive forces like?	Usually strong	Usually weak	Usually strong
What is strategy in this sector based on?	Competitive advantage	Public approval; competition for resources	Competitive advantage and stakeholder management
What is the language of strategy in this sector?	• Profit • Gaining market share	• Surplus • Providing a service	• Surplus • Acting for the social good

Chapter 2

Linking strategy to the market

Strategy has two dimensions: what is happening inside your organization and what is happening outside, in the market. You must understand and analyze both if you are to devise a successful strategy.

Looking ahead

Most people in an organization are constantly busy working to the next deadline. However, being driven by short-term goals should not preclude thinking about the future. A good manager always finds time to reflect upon where the business is going and whether its strategy remains valid.

Gaining first-mover advantage

Business is time precious. If you don't dispatch the order by Thursday, you'll lose the contract; if you don't complete your invoicing by the end of the quarter, you'll answer to your boss. A series of deadlines can stretch out far into the future, and it's all too easy to get mired in day-to-day delivery.

But looking beyond the "now" will help you avoid future troubles that may affect your business and will enable you to spot opportunities to achieve more sales, develop new services, and pre-empt your competitors' activities to gain first-mover advantage.

The attentive organization or team will soon gain advantage over the competition. For example, say you are a car manufacturer and you know that it takes five years to develop a new car design. If you receive early signals that taxation on large-engined cars will increase in five years, you can begin to develop smaller engines for your cars well before your competitors. Your product will emerge earlier than theirs and gain a strong foothold in a new market.

TIP

INVOLVE EVERYONE

Encourage and incentivize everyone in your team to be aware of what is going on in your organizational environment and find ways to collate any information they discover.

Knowing who is responsible

So whose job is it to watch out for hazards and opportunities and assess the potential effects of new competition and changes in the wider economy? Usually, strategy is seen as the preserve of a business's leaders, and while it's true that good strategists often achieve senior management positions, monitoring organizational strategy can, and should, involve people throughout the organization. Your salespeople, for example, may be best placed to gain information about the market (the best source of competitor knowledge is often your own customers). Similarly, your purchasing staff may have advance warning of price increases in key raw materials. Find ways to collect such knowledge and use it to inform your strategy.

✓ CHECKLIST **FOCUSING ON THE FUTURE**

	YES	NO
• Do I know what our customers (internal or external) are doing and what their future plans are?	☐	☐
• Do I know what our competitors are doing?	☐	☐
• Have I assessed whether there are any constraints that could affect our business in the next few years?	☐	☐
• Have I analyzed whether there are opportunities for my team?	☐	☐
• Do I know who is responsible for gathering information?	☐	☐

Analyzing your environment

To be effective, an organization needs to achieve some degree of match between what it can offer and what the world needs. Making sense of the complex environment in which you do business, and using this information to create good strategy, is essential if your business is to survive.

Using analysis tools

Analyzing the environment in which you operate is the first step to creating a strategy. There are a number of analysis tools that can help you assess your chosen market and also the world in which you do business:

Q IN FOCUS...
TRACKING YOUR MARKET

To understand the environment in which you do business, you must dedicate time to consciously seeking out the information you require. For example, to be a successful car dealer, you must buy the right cars at the right prices. To do this, you must spend time "in the market"—watching and listening for information about which cars are selling well or proving difficult to sell, and which cars are increasing in price or are decreasing in value. This requires casual observations, but also real data, such as week-to-week recording and analysis of car-price data, customer numbers, and stock levels. This combined approach allows you to create the right strategy for your business.

• **SWOT analysis** This can help you understand your organization and its market or environment, by contrasting its "Strengths" and "Weaknesses" with the "Opportunities" and "Threats" in the market.

• **PESTLE analysis** This assesses macroeconomic forces that affect all markets, including political and economic factors, social trends, and legislation.

• **Porter's 5 Forces (P5F)** This looks at factors that are operating within a given market, and that are of significance to all organizations within that market, but not necessarily other markets.

There may be some overlap in the information these tools generate, but it is still best to use all three, as each can generate unique information and insight.

Performing a SWOT analysis

TIP

SWOT analysis is a tool that can be used to generate an overview of an organization's position within a particular market, or a team's position within an organization. Use the SWOT matrix to determine and compare the internal strengths and weaknesses of your organization or team, and to analyze the opportunities for it and threats to it within the market. The information you collect will enable you to make decisions that could help to put your organization into a stronger position by making the most of your strengths, minimizing your weaknesses, exploiting the opportunities open to you in the market, and mitigating any threats.

USE YOUR RESULTS

If you've taken the time to analyze your situation using analysis tools, don't let the data you've collected just sit in a file—be sure to use the information to inform your strategy.

SWOT analysis for a team within an organization

	POSITIVE	
INTERNAL	**S**TRENGTHS Strengths of the team: • Generally, we are considered to have a good reputation within the organization. • We have received good financial support in the last two years. • Our processes are efficient.	**W**EAKNESSES Weaknesses of the team: • We have trouble recruiting staff in key team positions. • We are expensive relative to other related teams within the organization.
EXTERNAL	**O**PPORTUNITIES Opportunities in the market (the organization): • A related team within the organization has troubles and they could be merged into our team. • We could strengthen our role.	**T**HREATS Threats in the market (the organization): • The work of a related team has already been outsourced to an external company. • We have poor relations with some of our internal customers.

Looking at major forces

The macroeconomic forces that affect your organization, and your competitors, your markets, and even whole countries and the global economy, can have significant implications and are beyond your control. Given the scale of these forces, it is vital to identify and understand them so that you can use that knowledge to create good strategy.

HOW TO... DO A PESTLE ANALYSIS

Gather the team and brainstorm each factor in turn.

↓

List anything that could affect your organization in the future.

↓

Reconvene if more detailed knowledge is required.

↓

Narrow the list to the main factors that need to be considered when developing new strategy.

Using PESTLE analysis

The PESTLE analysis tool was developed to help identify and understand macroeconomic forces that may impact on an organization, such as global and national economic factors (for example, growth or recession), changes in technology, and emerging social trends, such as attitudes to climate change. PESTLE analysis divides these forces into six factors: political, economic, social, technological, legal, and environmental. It is also used in the abbreviated form PEST (or STEP).

A PESTLE analysis should be an early step in creating new strategy, because it sets out the background in which an organization has to operate and make decisions. It can be performed by an individual, but is often best undertaken by a team so that ideas can be shared and discussed. PESTLE can be set out on flipcharts or a whiteboard, especially when being done by a team, but there is also software available to do the analysis. You should be able to identify most PESTLE factors quickly, but you may need to spend time researching specific issues in more detail. This research is important, because strategic decisions must be based on the best data available at the time.

The output of your PESTLE analysis can be used in conjunction with SWOT analysis to explore further how the macroeconomic factors you have identified may impact on your organization.

The six PESTLE factors

POLITICAL
The impact of decisions made by government(s), from new laws and policies to political goals and ideologies, such as increasing gender equality.

ENVIRONMENTAL
The impact of consumer attitudes toward and legislation relating to environmental issues, such as pollution and climate change.

ECONOMIC
Issues related to the distribution, supply, and availability of money, such as the performance of national economies and changes in currency exchange rates.

LEGAL
The impact of existing laws, proposed changes to laws, or the introduction or removal of laws. These can be general laws or those specific to business.

SOCIAL
The impact of social factors, such as collective social belief of what is right or wrong, and changes in taste, fashion, attitudes, and work ethics.

TECHNOLOGICAL
The emergence and availability of new and enabling technologies—automation, for example—meaning new things are possible and old processes are obsolete.

Assessing the market

Analyzing the specific market in which your organization operates is key to making good strategic decisions. The Porter's 5 Forces (P5F) analysis tool can help you understand how competitive forces work within your chosen market, to analyze the behavior of your competitors and their impact on one another, and ultimately to achieve competitive advantage.

TIP

STAY UP TO DATE
A P5F analysis describes a competitive situation, which can change frequently, so ensure that your analysis is regularly updated to take into account the latest market conditions.

Understanding rivalry

The Porter's 5 Forces model was developed by American researcher and writer on strategy, Professor Michael Porter. At its heart is the concept of industry rivalry, or the degree of intensity of competition. Understanding this helps to define how attractive a market is to your organization: intense rivalry suggests too much competition and less opportunity for you to survive and be profitable.

Using Porter's 5 Forces

The model looks at five forces that define the market: how easy it is for new businesses to enter; how easy it is for customers to substitute your product or service for another; how much power suppliers and buyers in the market have; and the overall degree of competitive rivalry within the market.

Consider each of the five forces in turn. Start by assessing how difficult it is for you to enter the market. One aspect of competition is that if you are seen to be successful in a market, then others will quickly follow. It is more attractive, therefore, for a market to be easy for you to enter, but to have high barriers to entry for others. Next consider the second force: how easy it is for your customers to substitute your product or service with another.

PORTER'S 5 FORCES

FORCE	QUESTIONS
Potential entrants	• Does the market require you to have particular knowledge to be successful? If yes, it hinders others from entering. • How easy is it to set up in business in the market? Does it take a few hundred dollars or a few million dollars? • Is branding important in the market? If yes, then brand building may be a problem for new entrants.
Potential substitutes	• How easy is it for customers to switch to another type of product or service (to change from using a private car to a public train service, for example)?
Power of suppliers	• Where is the balance of power between suppliers and the firms in the market? Too much supplier power makes the market unattractive. • How easy is it to switch suppliers that offer an equivalent or superior product or service? (The easier, the better.)
Power of buyers	• Where is the balance of power between buyers and the firms in the market? Too much buyer power makes the market unattractive. • How many rivals do you have to supply your product or service? How easy would it be for your customer to drop you and use another?
Competitive rivalry	• Is there room in the market for all companies? If there is, particularly if the market is growing, then this increases the attractiveness. • Is the market contracting? If so, rivalry may be intense.

The power of buyers and suppliers are two sides of the same coin. If all the companies within the market need to buy a certain raw material, and there is only one supplier, this supplier has power over supply and pricing. Similarly, if one retailer controls the distribution and sale of a product, then that retailer (the buyer) has control. A market in which you have less control and power is not as attractive to enter as one in which you are not constrained in this way.

The first four factors combine to make an overall competitive rivalry, so the final step of the analysis is to consider how strong this is for your particular market.

The output of P5F analysis can be used in a SWOT analysis, to link this information about the market to the strengths and weaknesses of your organization.

Choosing your approach

When developing a strategy for the future of your business, you will be presented with a dilemma: should you focus on what you are good at, or on what other people want from you? When making your decision, remember that these two approaches are not mutually exclusive, and good strategies often involve a combination of the two.

Playing to your strengths

The "inside-out" approach to strategy involves looking at what you have that is of value to your organization and to the market—a shop in a busy location, for example. Known as "resources," these are the assets of your organization. However, resources alone are useless. It is how you use them—your competencies*—that will ultimately lead to your success or failure. For example, consider a fast-food business that has a busy city-center location. Such a business will not make money unless it combines its shop resource with staff who know how to deliver great food very quickly.

*Competencies—
the ways in which you turn your resources into activities that are valuable to your organization.

The inside-out approach is also known as the "resource-based view" of strategy, and is based on looking at your resources and competencies—what you are good at—and identifying markets that need them. Clearly playing to your strengths in this way makes a great deal of sense, but this strategy suffers one critical flaw: if no-one wants to buy what you are good at, then you have no viable business. This lack of market input into your activities means that an inside-out approach alone may not always be successful.

ASK YOURSELF...
WHAT RESOURCES DO WE HAVE?

- Does our location give us competitive advantage in any market?
- Do our staff have skills that our competitors lack?
- Do we have access to materials at a lower price than our competitors?
- Do we have technology or processes that could give us an advantage?

Meeting needs

The reverse approach is known as "outside-in," or a "market-based view" of strategy. This involves identifying what the customers and the market are going to need or want in the future, and then developing your resources and competencies to satisfy those market needs. This approach has the advantage of ensuring that your products or services are desired in this market and will be bought. However, it may be hard to succeed with this strategy if what the market wants is not what you are good at, and if it is not easy or is prohibitively expensive to acquire the relevant resources and competencies.

Striking a balance

In reality, a strategy that seeks to achieve a balance of the inside-out and outside-in approaches may be the most successful. There is no set formula for creating this balance—what matters is that it is right for your business. Consider, for example, an organization that owns a medium-sized hotel in its own grounds with a group of experienced staff. Its strategy might be to look at these resources and select the most lucrative market using them (hotels specializing in romantic breaks, for example). Once the hotel has identified this market, it might then modify its resources and competencies to optimize its success in serving it.

CASE STUDY

A balanced approach

As the 21st century approached, the German car manufacturer Volkswagen Audi Group realized that motor manufacturing was changing and that big international manufacturers would dominate the industry. However, it also knew that the bigger the organization, the more complex and expensive it is to run, and so it had to find a way to be both big and efficient. One way it achieved this was to realize that different markets would want different cars, and that expanding its operation to satisfy these markets would be operationally complex and stretch its resources. It used a balance of inside-out and outside-in approaches to create its strategy. It took the same car components (such as engines, controls, and wheels) and assembled them into very similar cars, using the same resources and competencies, but sold them to different customer groups using different brand names, such as Volkswagen, Audi, Seat, and Skoda. It balanced its knowledge of individual markets with an awareness of its own resources and competencies— and where it lacked certain resources (a brand for that territory, for example), it bought them so it had the right resources to serve that market's need.

Fitting or stretching

Your strategy is defined by the macroeconomic and market forces that continually act upon your organization. Doing nothing to respond to these forces is not an option, because without action their impact will ultimately destroy you. You have a choice: to "fit" within these forces, or to employ a "stretch" strategy that could lead to growth in the future.

Achieving "fit"

Picture your organization surrounded by its competitors and forces in the market, and by the macroeconomic forces that impact on all organizations. These forces push at your organization from all sides and can, in time, crush it. If your organization responds by making decisions and taking actions—such as selling new products or moving into new markets—it will push back against these crushing forces. It will become stronger and if its forces are equal to the forces pushing it, then it will maintain itself and we can say that it has achieved "fit." This means that effectively standing still requires active management; and

IN FOCUS... THE ANSOFF MATRIX

The Ansoff Matrix is a tool that can help define the options open to a business when deciding on a strategy for selling their products. The matrix lists four possible options, ordered by how much risk is involved, from least to most risky:
• To sell existing products or services into existing markets
• To sell new products or services to existing markets (i.e., to sell new products to the same customers)
• To sell existing products or services to new markets
• To sell new products or services to new markets.
When choosing which of these strategies to use to sell your products, consider your existing resources and competencies, taking into account how easy it would be for you to develop or acquire any that you currently lack, and the level of risk involved in undertaking each option.

achieving "fit" cannot happen by doing nothing. The concept of "fit" reflects the fact that all organizations operate in a dynamic environment. If you decide to begin work at 9 am, for example, there is no reason why your competitors cannot decide to start at 8 am. Even if you decide that you want your team or organization to remain roughly the same, at the very least your costs will grow every year, which means you need to earn more to cover them; and in addition your competitors and your markets are likely to change. So, whatever your business, you can never afford to stand still: a strategy for achieving "fit" is the minimum requirement.

TIP

TAKE ADVICE
Talk to people both inside and outside your organization to explore whether a "fit" or a "stretch" strategy would be right for you.

Planning for growth

In many circumstances you may want to go further than simply "fitting" within your market, and attempt to make yourself more dominant. A "stretch" strategy is an extension of "fit," and involves making decisions and taking actions that enable you to grow, and in doing so push your competitors back or even crush them. A "stretch" approach, if successful, puts you in a stronger position, and may perhaps mean that your organization lives longer. However, you must also weigh up that employing a "stretch" strategy means that the scale of decisions and actions you have to take will be greater, so it is likely to consume more time and resources and involve a higher level of risk than a "fit" strategy.

Choosing your customers

If you take the time to review and analyze your customers, you will find that they are not equally valuable: some will produce strong, continuous, reliable forms of income, while others give you small pieces of complex work, argue over what you have done, and then are slow to pay you. A good strategy aims to identify and target customers with characteristics that are most beneficial to your organization.

Attracting the right customers

In the early stages of a business, it is natural to say "yes" to all potential customers. You may be under financial pressures to earn income, and want to seek reassurances that you are doing a good job and that people want to work with you. However, some customers have characteristics that give them the potential to be much more beneficial to your organization than others.

Possible characteristics of good customers

FINANCIALLY BENEFICIAL
They provide you with regular profitable income; they are willing to pay a higher-than-average price; they give you a large volume of work so it improves your turnover figures; they pay promptly and it improves your cash flow.

Take time to think about the characteristics that would most benefit your organization. If you can identify customers with those characteristics and find ways to attract them, you will gain the double benefit of having the customers that you want and sending the less beneficial customers to your competitors, so that they waste their time, not yours.

Once you have determined the types of customers you want and don't want, target your marketing to your preferred groups. For example, if you have decided that large customers are more beneficial to your organization than small ones, don't place your advertisements in local community magazines—advertise in national media. Strategic marketing of your products to attract the right customers also extends to pricing: if you price your products very low, you may attract only the most cost-conscious customers, who are likely to argue over price.

TIP

REVIEW YOUR CUSTOMERS

Regularly look through your customer list and ask yourself: what is the compelling reason for having this customer?

KNOWLEDGE ENHANCING
They provide valuable insight into areas that you are not familiar with, such as a new market sector or a new country that would be strategically important for your organization.

REPUTATION ENHANCING
Their custom enhances your reputation in the market. For example, if you write software for the financial services industry and a major Wall Street firm buys your software, other customers will assume that you must be good.

STRUCTURE ENHANCING
They enable you to invest in new resources: for example, if a potential but not well-paying customer would provide work to fill 60 percent of an expensive new machine's capacity, that customer's work would allow you to invest in a key new resource.

Avoiding competition

Competition, by its very nature, means that there will be winners and losers—and in the competition for customers, those that fail to gain a competitive advantage in the market will ultimately fail altogether. A good strategy, therefore, should include finding ways to avoid competition.

Understanding competition

Competition can be a destructive force for your organization. Consider two coffee shops that are situated next to one another, and that offer a similar standard of coffee and service. Both of the shops are suffering poor sales. To try to boost its performance, one of the shops decides to offer a 10-percent discount on all orders. This is successful, and attracts more customers to the shop. In response, the second coffee shop introduces a 15-percent discount, in turn winning more of the local business, and putting pressure on the first shop to offer an even larger discount. This pattern of behavior is likely to ultimately lead to the destruction of both shops. All markets go through this destructive competitive process, which leads—in time—to the failure of many competitors and the dominance of a very small number of the most competitive players.

Positioning yourself

The two coffee shops could avoid competition by targeting different kinds of customers rather than fighting over the same ones. One could choose to supply lower-quality take-out coffee that would appeal to those on a budget, while the other could provide more upmarket coffees and pastries in a stylish café to appeal to those with more income. In this way, by

Segment—a subgroup within the market that more precisely defines a group of customers. For example, within the car market, segments include parents with young children, who want larger family cars, and others looking for a small "city car" as a second vehicle.

actively targeting different customers to your competitors and choosing to serve only one market segment*, you can reduce the destructive forces of competition. If you are successful and develop a dominant position in your chosen market segment, competitors may be intimidated and look for their own segment to move into.

Assessing positions

A basic way to look at strategic positioning within a market is to position brands on a scale from low to high quality and price. The example below maps out how a number of car brands might position themselves in a typical national market. Each has chosen to focus on particular market segments, and so reduce the number of competitors they have. Brand C, for example, sells budget-range cars at the lower end of the price scale and so avoids competition with brands that are targeting customers with more money to spend.

Strategic positioning of car brands within a market

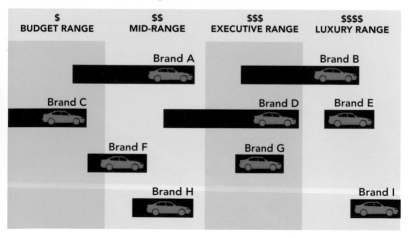

$ BUDGET RANGE	$$ MID-RANGE	$$$ EXECUTIVE RANGE	$$$$ LUXURY RANGE
	Brand A		Brand B
Brand C		Brand D	Brand E
	Brand F	Brand G	
	Brand H		Brand I

Three generic strategies

A business strategy is unique to the organization and environment in which it operates. However, research conducted by Professor Michael Porter recognizes three generic organizational strategies that businesses use to gain and maintain competitive advantage within a market: cost leadership, differentiation, and focus. Each requires a particular philosophical approach to be applied throughout the whole organization.

TIP

PREVENT STRATEGY DRIFT

You can choose to pursue one of the three strategies in its pure form or to devise a hybrid. If you do the latter, monitor the strategy regularly to ensure its clarity and integrity—a hybrid can easily drift into compromise.

Focusing on cost

Cost-leadership strategy positions an organization as the lowest-cost producer in a particular industry. Everything about the firm is designed to be low cost—labor, premises, materials, capital, and so on. The firm's products or services are comparable in quality and price to the rest of the market: profit comes from the difference between the low costs and the market price. A subdivision of the cost-leadership strategy is the "no-frills" strategy, where low-cost production is still sought but the products or services are acknowledged to be of more basic quality.

Adding benefits

Differentiation strategy is a near-opposite approach to cost leadership. A firm employing this strategy adds additional features to its products or services to make them above average in the market. For example, where a no-frills airline may offer little airport support (or make passengers pay extra for it), a differentiating airline may include a limo to the airport and a private lounge in the price of its tickets. Key factors for success with a differentiation strategy are that customers must desire the extra features and be willing to pay a price premium for them. The cost of providing the extras must be less than the price premium they are prepared to pay.

Being a specialist

Focus strategy involves an organization concentrating on one particular market or market niche and becoming expert in that area. Customers buy from that organization because they are the best in that field. A focus strategy for an airline, for example, may be to fly only business-class passengers in private jets. There are many examples of focus strategy being used to great effect: German car manufacturer Porsche, for example, focuses only on sports cars and has a global reputation for doing so. However, focus strategy also carries more risk, because you are building up resources and competencies in only one narrow area.

COMPARING THE THREE STRATEGIES

STRATEGY	ADVANTAGES	DISADVANTAGES
Cost leadership Being the lowest-cost producer in the industry	Can be easy to implement	Can be difficult to sustain—you are vulnerable to being undercut by your competitors
Differentiation Providing "extras" to your product or service desired by your customers	Premium pricing can mean more money is available for activities that maintain the advantage, such as R&D	The source of differentiation can become stale over time and new "extras" need to be developed
Focus Concentrating on one smaller part of the market and becoming expert and dominant in it	Can give very high profit margins and lead to a market-dominating position	Risky: market niche may change or disappear; if you are successful, big firms may try to muscle in on your market

Chapter 3

Creating a good strategy

You know your market, are sure of your objectives, and understand your options. What you need now is to evaluate those options and create a vision, a plan to achieve it, and a clear understanding of how to make that plan work.

Setting the priorities

You need to consider many factors when drafting your strategy. Your responsibilities to your stakeholders, to your stated ethical principles and mission, and to society in general are important, but are ultimately subservient to return on investment (or the effective use of resources for non-profit organizations). So what does a good strategy look like?

Defining the ingredients

Every successful strategy presents a vision and a plan for creating and maintaining competitive advantage in the future. It asks, and answers, questions such as:
• What services or products will be required in the next three to five years?
• Who will your competitors be?
• Why will you be more successful than them?
This vision will need the support of others in order to achieve its goals, and so must be compatible with the demands of your stakeholders. Some of these

individuals and groups will have a direct interest in your strategy (for example, your staff, higher managers, and funders), while others—such as shareholders and pressure groups—may have an indirect interest. You will need to identify and obtain support from your most important stakeholders—some of whom will help you implement the strategy—if your strategy is to be successful. For example, the principal of a school has to take into account the views of pupils, parents (current and future), staff, financiers, regulatory authorities, the local community, and competitors (anticipating how they may react) when making strategic decisions.

Finally, your strategy must be capable of being implemented. There is no shortage in the business world of overambitious strategies languishing in filing cabinets. While a good strategy must be challenging, leading the organization into the future, it must also be understandable, practical, and rooted in reality.

Putting it in writing

When planning your strategy, it can be useful to write your ideas down. The discipline of producing a written, well-reasoned document helps to focus your mind on the questions you need to address and produces a record against which you can check your progress. It also allows others to scrutinize the strategy, which can be very helpful—if you ask a few trusted and knowledgeable colleagues for their opinions, they will often see things from a different perspective and may unlock new possibilities that hadn't occurred to you.

There is no formula for how a written strategy should be presented—every organization is different—but there are a few key points that it should address. Make sure that what you write is both believable and motivational in tone.

HOW TO...
PREPARE A WRITTEN STRATEGY

Describe what your organization does.

Set out what the future world you will face looks like.

Describe your sustainable competitive advantage.

State why you will be in a strong position compared with your competitors.

Define milestones of achievement, so you can monitor your progress.

Evaluating your options

Many managers develop a sixth sense for the market, and make strategic decisions based largely on instinct. However, even after you have worked in a particular industry for many years, you should always evaluate any decisions you make with a degree of objectivity.

THINK ABOUT ALL POSSIBILITIES
Work hard to identify your options—you may discover a less-obvious opportunity that could be successful after a careful evaluation of the possibilities open to you.

Developing alternatives

When you create or review your strategy, it is likely that you will have many preconceptions about where the business should go, and it is all too easy to believe that your first solution is the right one. In reality, your range of strategic options is likely to be very wide—from continuing with business as usual, through to fundamental and revolutionary changes.

You will already have gathered information about your organization and its environment. Start by developing a number of options based on this information—some innovative and adventurous, some more conservative. Include the "do nothing" option as a baseline. These options should be based on your sound research—the key threats and opportunities you face; your strengths and weaknesses; and the expectations of management and other stakeholders.

Using consistent criteria

Next, assess how valuable each of the options is to your organization by testing each one against some consistent criteria. You can devise your own set of criteria, but it may be better to rely on established measures. For example, a classic work on strategic management by Johnson, Scholes, and Whittington sets out three criteria for evaluating strategic options: suitability, acceptability, and feasibility.

HOW TO... **PLAN AND EVALUATE STRATEGIC OPTIONS**

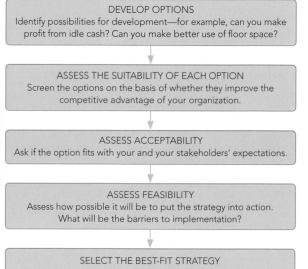

GATHER INFORMATION
Analyze your resources and competencies. Look at the business environment—growth, market structures, and the broader economy.

DEVELOP OPTIONS
Identify possibilities for development—for example, can you make profit from idle cash? Can you make better use of floor space?

ASSESS THE SUITABILITY OF EACH OPTION
Screen the options on the basis of whether they improve the competitive advantage of your organization.

ASSESS ACCEPTABILITY
Ask if the option fits with your and your stakeholders' expectations.

ASSESS FEASIBILITY
Assess how possible it will be to put the strategy into action. What will be the barriers to implementation?

SELECT THE BEST-FIT STRATEGY

TIP

MAKE A FAIR ASSESSMENT
Consider each option objectively and honestly even if you have a favourite—remember, the strategy you are choosing now is likely to be one that you follow for many years, so you have to get the decision right.

Assessing suitability

Suitability measures how well a strategic option provides a good fit between your organization and its environment, now and in the future. To assess the suitability of an option, ask yourself questions such as:
• Will it get us to where we want to be in the future?
• Does it achieve the right balance between what we are good at and what the market wants?
• How will it impact on the organization?
   Each option that passes the suitability test should then be considered for its acceptability and feasibility.

Assessing acceptability

Acceptability refers to whether a strategic option is likely to give worthwhile results for the key stakeholders—usually management, shareholders, employees, and customers. This includes not just acceptable financial return, but also less quantifiable factors, such as risk (the impact on your brand's reputation, for example) and value to stakeholders. It is likely that you will be unable to please all stakeholders, so you will need to decide who are the most important. To assess the acceptability of a strategic option, ask yourself questions such as:
• Will the financial return be acceptable?
• What are the risks of the option, and are they acceptable?
• How will this option affect each stakeholder group, and is this outcome acceptable?
• Will this option give the right balance of cost and benefits?

Assessing feasibility

Feasibility addresses whether it is within your power and capabilities to implement a strategic option. Strategic change requires time, effort, and money (TEM), so make a realistic assessment of your ability to make it happen by asking questions such as:
• Is sufficient funding available? You may be a small team that could deliver a great new service if you have a million dollars, but is it possible for you to access that funding?
• Do we have the time available?
• Do we have the skills in-house (or could we access them) to make this option happen?
• Does your organizational culture support the change? Your management may be highly risk averse, for example, and block radical plans.

Q IN FOCUS... REMAINING OBJECTIVE

It can be hard to remain objective when deciding upon strategy. The final outcome is so important to the future of the organization that other factors, such as personalities and power politics within the organization, inevitably have a strong influence on the strategy you opt for. However, it is your responsibility to elevate the process beyond the personal agendas or opinions of stakeholders. Try to raise the level of debate by using objective scoring systems so that everyone can see the relative merits of each option. Calling in external consultants can help to free up objective thinking and help overcome barriers or inertia.

Scoring the options

To test each of your strategic options against the criteria of suitability, acceptability, and feasibility, it helps to develop a simple scoring system rather than simply assigning a "yes" or "no." Mark each option on a scale of one to 10 for each of the criteria, being honest and objective in your scoring. Add the scores for suitability, acceptability, and feasibility for each option to identify the best.

Reading the future

Strategy is simple: just work out what the world will be like in five years and organize your resources and competencies to achieve a match. However, this raises the vital question—how do you know what the world will look like in five years? No one can see what is to come, but there are techniques that will help you visualize and plan for the future.

The tools

Analysis tools, such as SWOT, PESTLE, and Porter's 5 Forces, are excellent for describing your current market(s) and business environment. Extrapolating beyond the present, however, is far more difficult, but is nonetheless essential when planning strategy. Two useful tools—forecasting and scenario planning—can help with this task.

Using forecasting

Forecasting is the process of predicting the future based upon past and present trends. For example, if your salary bill has increased by a consistent three percent per annum for the previous 10 years, you can realistically extrapolate the rise for the next two years. You can also carry out more sophisticated forecasts based on intelligence. For example, you may know that your sales are strongly influenced both by a

competitor's activity and by consumer price inflation.

By gaining intelligence on your competitors' projected activity, and economists' predictions of inflation, you can make an informed forecast of next year's sales. Forecasting works only when you make realistic and honest assumptions about your business and its environment.

Painting scenarios

Some factors move unpredictably, so it is not possible to use historical data to predict future movements. For these, scenario planning is more appropriate. This form of planning involves painting alternative scenes—images of your future business environment—and assessing how your organization would fare in each circumstance. A classic case is the price of oil, which fluctuates in response to a complex mix of political, financial, and production factors. One scenario envisages oil prices remaining stable over three years; another has prices at 150 percent of current levels; and a third has them at 75 percent. How would your business be affected by each? How will each influence your strategy?

Involving stakeholders

Stakeholders are individuals or organizations that have an interest in how your organization is run. The ready availability of information, especially through the media and the internet, means that stakeholders have an increasingly strong voice, and some may seek to influence your strategy. It is vital, therefore, to identify and manage your most important stakeholders.

Analyzing impacts

While all of the stakeholders in your organization are important, not all will have equal impact upon you. Stakeholder mapping is a tool that can help you identify and manage the stakeholders that are most influential in your business. Start by identifying every stakeholder that has an interest in your organization. Then look at the names on your list:

PRESSURE GROUPS
May put their cause above your future

• Determine each stakeholder's level of interest in your activities
• Assess their level of power over your organization
• Identify who are the most powerful and the most interested stakeholders.
Use this information to assess how important stakeholders will respond to different strategic options, and to plan how to influence them.

Balancing interests

Managing multiple stakeholders can often present a dilemma. For example, your investors want you to always be seeking to reduce costs, while your employees want to receive higher salaries. When making decisions that affect multiple stakeholders, use the information you have gathered in your analysis to assess the balance of power, and consider this against your values and those of the organization.

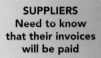

INDUSTRY ASSOCIATIONS
Set standards and best practices

MEDIA
Has the power to influence many, for good and for bad

INVESTORS
Want to know that their money is safe in your hands

COMMUNITY
Are a source of the staff and support you need

SUPPLIERS
Need to know that their invoices will be paid

Possible stakeholders in your organization

EMPLOYEES
Want their loyalty and productivity to be rewarded

GOVERNMENT
Can provide mutual support that may be a source of power

CUSTOMERS
Will decide whether they want to be associated with you

TRADE UNIONS
Require their members to be treated well

COMPETITORS
Act in ways that may affect your options and influence your decisions

Linking strategy to structure

Having developed your options, it is important to consider how your organization would implement a selected strategy. Part of addressing this is deciding whether the organization is structured in the right way to support the new strategy, or whether, despite all good intentions, the old organizational structure will lead to its failure.

Analyzing your structure

Should strategy drive structure or should structure drive strategy? Strategy is clearly more important than structure, because by implementing a new strategy your team or organization can create the future. It is clear, therefore, that strategy must come first—an organization must create the right strategy and then adjust its structure to ensure that the chosen strategy has the greatest chance of success.

Consider the existing structure of your organization. This is most easily visualized by creating a staff diagram. Start with the most senior person at the top of your organization and then work downward through the hierarchy. The teams or groups in your organization are represented horizontally. Link each group using lines to represent the lines of communication between them.

✔ CHECKLIST **FINDING THE BEST FIT**

	YES	NO
• Can you change your company structure to better support your chosen strategy?	☐	☐
• Can you change your company structure in the longer term to open up more strategic options?	☐	☐
• As a last resort, can your strategy be changed or amended to better align it with your company structure?	☐	☐

Making changes

Now think about how this structure would affect the implementation of your strategy. For example, consider an organization whose structure is complex with many layers. Decisions need to be approved at each level, making decision-making slow. This makes it difficult for the organization to respond to market changes, and so adopt a market-based view of strategy. To be successful, the structure needs to be simplified. If the CEO and general manager, for example, give authority to business units within the organization to manage their own affairs, each business unit is able to make decisions rapidly and respond to the market.

However, restructuring such as this may not always be possible, and even if it is, it will take time, effort, and money. In these cases, a compromise can often be the best solution: first make your best effort to change the structure to support the strategy; if you cannot change it entirely, determine how you could modify the strategy to do the best you can within existing structural constraints.

Restructuring the organization for decision-making efficiency

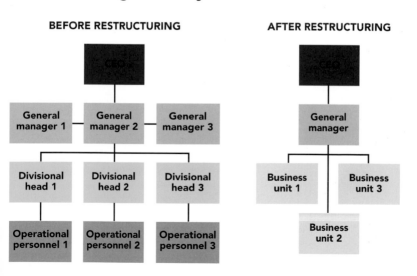

BEFORE RESTRUCTURING

- CEO
  - General manager 1
    - Divisional head 1
      - Operational personnel 1
  - General manager 2
    - Divisional head 2
      - Operational personnel 2
  - General manager 3
    - Divisional head 3
      - Operational personnel 3

AFTER RESTRUCTURING

- CEO
  - General manager
    - Business unit 1
    - Business unit 2
    - Business unit 3

Knowing when to change

Time is a critical factor in making strategic decisions. When should you make strategic changes, and how is your strategy influenced by the time you have available? The key is to always remain flexible: although strategy is about the future, the time to act may be now.

Getting the timing right

Many teams and organizations review their strategy only when things are going wrong—if all's well, why change? This is false logic: in fact, the best time to plan for change is precisely when you have morale, time, profits, and momentum on your side. Strategic change might mean making a large investment, relocating a business, merging with a competitor, taking on new staff, or engaging with new markets. Big changes such as this take time, so it is vital to consider timescales in your strategic planning. For example, you may decide to merge with a competitor because they have good sales in territories that complement your own. Strategically this makes sense. However, it may take months of negotiation to agree the merger, another few months to conclude the legal and financial aspects of the deal, and even longer to merge the systems and staff of the two organizations. So your relatively simple idea may take 18 months or more to execute—great if you have that amount of time available, but if your need is to generate additional sales in the current financial year you will need to look for an alternative approach.

Reacting to events

In reality, despite the best intentions to plan for all eventualities, the unexpected does happen and you may need to devise a strategy quickly in reaction to changed circumstances. Without the benefit of time, your options for change are likely to be limited. You need to acknowledge these limits—how much time you actually have—and then work backwards to develop strategic options that fit the parameters.

BE READY TO CHANGE
Avoid being pushed into a corner with limited options—always be alert to your changing environment to give yourself plenty of time to make changes.

First, quantify the urgency of the situation—how long do you have to make the change? Next, identify the key issues you face and place them in order of priority. For example, in a small company you may identify that poor teamwork has ultimately led to shortfalls in performance; lower revenues and recent investment in new equipment have left you vulnerable to creditors; and you may even face bankruptcy. In this situation, a two-part strategic plan is necessary—part one addresses the immediate threat by stemming the losses and improving cash flow, and part two deals with the working practices and personnel issues that caused the problem.

TIMING STRATEGIC CHANGE

⬆ FAST TRACK	❗ OFF TRACK
Looking to surprise your competitors	Waiting to see what your competitors do before changing your strategy
Looking to spot early signals that change might be needed	Leaving "changing strategy" on your long-term to-do list
Thinking about your next strategic move when you are doing well	Taking success as a cue to rest on your laurels

TIP

BE OPEN
Sometimes experience isn't your best friend. Keep an open mind and don't become overconfident in your knowledge of the business and the marketplace: you could overlook vital signals.

Keeping alert

Strategy must adapt to new realities and to new forecasts: but exactly when should you make changes to your strategy? Should you do this at fixed, regular intervals or just when you deem it necessary?

In fact, no matter how solid your strategy, you must always be on the alert to make changes. Even if your strategy does not include seeking first-mover advantage, you must never be the last to realize that the world has changed while you have stood still.

The signals for change come from all around and are always out there—within your organization, the actions of your customers and competitors and changes in the market, and the macroeconomic climate. Make sure that you and your team have a good knowledge of these indicators for change, and encourage your team to always be on the lookout for potential warning signs and any other changes to your business environment. Put in place mechanisms by which information about these signals can be captured, communicated, and discussed.

Signals to change

- Fall or growth in sales
- Changes in the buying behavior of clients
- Media reports of macroeconomic change
- Changes in ease of staff recruitment
- Growth or contraction of competitors
- Shifts in regulation or government policy
- Changes in your supply chain
- Fall or growth in profits

Acting or not acting?

Having detected signs that you need to change, make sure that there is a strong case for doing so before you launch into changing your strategy. Weigh up the risks of changing against the risks of standing still, and don't succumb to strategy overload*—you are likely to disorientate your customers as well as your staff. Remember, too, that the costs of change—in terms of time, effort, and money—are high, and must be borne alongside the costs of running the business "as usual." Can you afford to make a change now? Or can you not afford to not change? Consider your options carefully before you make a decision.

*Strategy overload —changing strategic direction too often, or in response to small perturbations.

There are times when doing nothing is a viable option—but this must always be a conscious decision rather than one made by default or because it is the easier option. If you run a small business and are approaching retirement age, for example, you may make the perfectly legitimate decision that the time, effort, and money required to change strategy may not be worthwhile and it is better to maximize income within existing resources while the business slowly runs down.

CASE STUDY

Finding life beyond oil

In the early 21st century, companies and some countries involved in the oil industry are changing their strategies. Why? What are the signals that can help explain this? Firstly, the time at which oil reserves will run out is coming closer. Secondly, the impact on the earth's climate of carbon dioxide emissions generated by using oil will, for political, economic, social, and legislative reasons, lead to alternatives to oil being sought. Oil companies need a future, so for them (and for some oil-rich countries) developing new strategies away from oil provides a sustainable future. Why now? Because importantly they now have the time, effort, and money to achieve strategic change through investing in and developing new business opportunities, be it alternative energy, or investing in other companies or other ventures. These strategies are minor activities compared with the core business that remains focused on oil, but the aim is to insure those companies' futures. Is the time right for you to consider a new strategy?

Working with others

You may sometimes find that, after extensive analysis and planning, the best strategic option open to you is one that you are unable to implement alone, because you lack specific resources or competencies. In these cases, it may be possible to work together with another organization or group—even one of your competitors.

Exploring partnership

There are many types of relationship that you can establish with another organization, distinguished broadly by the degree of closeness.

At one end of the spectrum is some form of non-contractual trust-based relationship. You cooperate with another company in the market, but you occupy one niche, they another; you support one another in your weaker areas and so can bid for work larger than

DIFFERENT FORMS OF STRATEGIC RELATIONSHIPS

TYPE	ADVANTAGES	DISADVANTAGES
Trust-based	Flexible	No contractual basis
	Able to change quickly in response to the market	Based on a relationship that could turn sour
Contractual	Formalized	Difficult to exit
Joint venture	Clear about nature of resources and competencies gained/given	May lose key knowledge
	Not necessarily constrained by the cultures of the partner organizations	May develop a life of its own that conflicts with the partner organizations
	Moves financial risk into another company	May lead to power struggles

you could on your own. Trust-based relationships may emerge between smaller companies that have complementary expertise, and often between business owners who have built their businesses over many years and who know and respect one another.

In the middle are relationships characterized by formal agreements, in which the roles are more precisely defined. In the eyes of your customers, you may be seen as one or two organizations. Such contractual relationships take a number of forms, including subcontracting, where one party delivers a defined service to another, or outsourcing arrangements, where one party takes over a specific role for the partner business (providing administrative, personnel, or IT services, for example).

At the other end of the scale is a joint venture or consortium, in which the two (or more) organizations come together to create something with its own identity. A joint venture might involve companies A and B creating a new business: company C. Both A and B put money, staff, and other resources into company C, which, importantly, has its own management.

KNOW THE SCORE

Remember that a partnership is a form of "trade." You will usually have to give up some of your power and control, so be very sure that the trade is worthwhile before entering into any agreements.

Forging links

If you consider entering into a relationship with another organization to realize your strategy, you need to be sure that you will be gaining at least as much as you are giving, and that you are gaining something that you could not have achieved alone. Working closely with another group invariably has its pitfalls. You will be sharing potentially valuable knowledge with them, so you must consider where the boundaries of cooperation will lie, and how you will keep them secure. Where will power lie within the relationship? Is there a sense of equality, or will your partner wish to dominate? Is there enough trust and respect between you to enable an effective working relationship?

Chapter 4

Implementing your strategy

However well you have planned your strategy, if you make mistakes or are indecisive during implementation it will have little chance of success. You must lead your team confidently into a new future, keeping track of your progress along the way.

Demonstrating leadership

As in every aspect of life, there is often a natural resistance to change when you implement a new strategy. Change is a process that has to be led, so it is important that you develop leadership skills that will help you guide your organization and team through to a successful outcome.

LOOK TO THE MASTERS

Look at leaders you admire and make a list of what you can learn from them.

Defining good leadership

In the past, leaders were defined by their characteristics—such as confidence, intelligence, and being an expert. Much leadership training was based upon developing these traits. However, while these are traits that recognized leaders do exhibit, many are rather generic and difficult to measure and develop. Recent thinking defines leaders not by the characteristics that they have, but by what they do. Rather than having a set style of leadership, an effective leader analyzes every situation (the context) and then adopts appropriate behaviors.

By definition, a leader is a leader of people (managers by comparison tend to manage processes) and can only be effective if those he or she is leading choose to follow. A good leader, therefore, must develop strong followership* amongst others.

*Followership— *an emotional commitment to the person who is leading you.*

Everyone can become a better leader. Leadership skills can be developed through coaching and training, but ultimately your capability to lead others will develop through practice and experience.

Leading in difficult times

Of course, it isn't that difficult to be a leader when times are good. Leaders earn their money when things are not going so well—when income is falling, staff are not working well and are leaving, and competitors are overtaking you. Changing strategy involves making significant changes, and this can often make things worse before it makes things better. At these times, people will be looking to you for reassurance that you are taking them on the right path.

LEADING THROUGH CHANGE

FAST TRACK	OFF TRACK
Being approachable and visible to those you are leading	Spending most of your time behind your closed office door
Inspiring confidence in your ability amongst those you are leading	Giving the impression of being indecisive or weak
Focusing on the context of any situation and adopting appropriate behaviors	Sounding negative or unenthusiastic, or lacking in a sense of purpose

Achieving cultural fit

It is easy to assume that we are all the same; that we all perceive the world in the same way, and that we will all make and understand the same decisions. As a leader of strategic change, it is important to recognize that there are significant cultural differences, and to consider these differences when creating and implementing your strategy.

Understanding different views

The way every individual sees the world is based on many things, including the country in which they were born and raised, their family and society, and their experiences. This "culture" becomes so ingrained that it may sometimes not even occur to you that other people see things differently in a particular context. This is of significant importance as you plan and deliver strategic change, as a lack of understanding of cultural differences can impact on your relationships with people and your attitude to change.

Cultural differences are not limited to differences between nations, although this is a key component. However, cultural differences can also be found between different sectors, such as between local government and small businesses. In addition, each organization has its own particular culture, and there can even be differences within organizations; the finance and marketing departments of an organization, for example, often have very different outlooks and values.

Understanding the culture of other people significantly improves your effectiveness in communication with them. This is particularly important in an external context, such as in your dealings with customers, in national and international markets. However, it also impacts within an organizational context, through your interactions with staff, colleagues, and managers.

Defining national differences

One of the most significant writers on national culture, Professor Geert Hofstede, has sought to define and measure national cultures, to provide greater insight into how people of different cultures behave in the workplace. Information such as this is useful to the strategic manager, particularly when developing new international markets and managing diverse workforces. Hofstede's work looked at differences in how societies accept equality or inequality; how they view risk; whether the individual or the group is considered to be most important; the strength of traditional male roles in a society; and whether there is an expectation that hard work now will be rewarded in the future.

IN FOCUS... CULTURAL DIFFERENCES

Hofstede's work drew some general conclusions about the characteristics of different cultures, including that:
• Eastern countries are more likely than Western countries to accept inequality within society (i.e., there are tiers within society and movement between them may be difficult).
• The group (the family or the team, for example) dominates Eastern societies, but Western countries (particularly the US and UK) more highly rate the individual.
• Scandinavian countries are characterized by their low level of gender discrimination.
• Western countries tend to want reward now; Eastern countries tend to take a longer-term view of reward.
  Remember that these differences are not about being right or wrong—they are the way things are.

Preparing others for change

Your role as a manager during change is to make it happen. This is far easier to achieve if you support your staff and take them with you on this journey. As you implement your strategy, spend time helping everyone who will be affected by the change understand and prepare for it.

Managing change

One issue to remember is that you and other management (especially senior management) may have been working on the need for change for some time. In your minds, it is clear why it should happen. For other staff, a strategy for change may come as a complete surprise. To mitigate adverse reactions it is important that, even if they don't like the change, your staff fully understand why it is necessary. Take the time to explain this. Also remember that with the journey you are taking them on, things may get worse before they get better. If people are going to follow someone on such a journey they must have confidence in the leader. Be that confident leader, and demonstrate that you are confident in your actions. Make yourself visible and available—this is no time to hide.

IN FOCUS... UNDERSTANDING RESPONSES TO CHANGE

Individuals perceive time differently. Listen to people around you, and you will find that some are always talking about tomorrow (future orientated); some are more focused on today and what is happening now; while others spend most time talking about the past. Individuals with each of these personality types perceive the need for change differently. This difference can be exaggerated by the scale of change: some people will be relatively relaxed about their job moving to another country, for example, while some will be anxious about moving their desk into another office.

Analyzing responses

Forcefield analysis is a tool that can help you understand the issues that may facilitate or hinder change, allowing you to look at solutions before problems arise. If your staff raise any of these issues you will be better prepared to deal with them. For example, the forcefield analysis below is for the relocation of company offices. Brainstorm a similar list of forces against your proposed change—reasons why individuals may be opposed to it—and a second list of reasons why they may be in favor of the change. Represent each negative force with an arrow pointing from right to left, and each positive force with an arrow pushing back at these forces from left to right. It can also be useful to adjust the size of the arrows to represent the relative size of each force. This analysis can help you identify the forces you need to focus on. Your aim should be to develop an action plan to maximize the forces for and reduce the forces against the change to drive it forward.

Forcefield analysis of a relocation

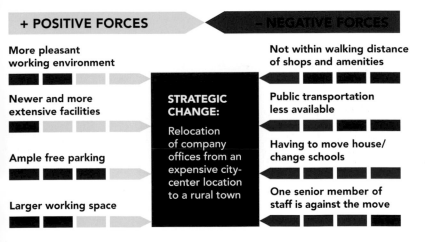

**HOW TO...
KEEP THE
TEAM IN
THE LOOP**

Determine what information each individual or group will need to know.

Decide when they will need to know it.

Choose the most effective means to communicate that information.

Choose the right person to deliver the information.

Record these details in a communication plan.

Communicate the details of the plan clearly to your team.

Reassuring your team

Implementing change inevitably means that your organization or team undergoes a period of uncertainty, which can make people feel unsettled and anxious. By its very nature, strategic change means the organization will stop doing some things and begin doing new, unfamiliar things. At first, the new tasks will not be natural and will take longer; and more mistakes will be made. It is important to reassure your team at this unsettling time, or they may begin to express their doubts in the direction you are taking them. Your role is to not have doubts (at least in public), and to keep telling your team members about how the changes will benefit them as well as the organization. The more difficult things become, the more reassurance they need from you.

Communicating effectively

One way to ease concern and guide your team is to have an effective communication plan. This is a set of "instructions" for exactly how you will disseminate information about your strategy and its implementation to all relevant parties. It can be difficult to keep everyone happy all of the time, but one thing that you must always bear in mind is that what your team members will object to most is hearing important news that affects them personally from others (and even worse through the media). This doesn't mean you have to (or should) do all of the communicating personally, but it is important to spend time identifying the key information that you must communicate yourself. In addition, identify the most important things to be communicated in person, by you or another member of the team. Other less important things can be communicated in other ways, such as by memo or email.

COMMUNICATING EFFECTIVELY

FAST TRACK

OFF TRACK

Planning how you will communicate different types of information to each party in advance	Thinking that you don't need a communication plan because you'll know what to do at the time
Being consistent in the facts you give to different groups	Giving mixed messages about the reasons behind the change
Changing your communication style to match the needs of the audience	Adopting a "one size fits all" model of communication

Balancing your responsibilities

As you implement your strategy, it is important to ensure that you make enough time in your day-to-day work for guiding your team through what may be choppy waters. However, leading those who are implementing your strategy and delivering change can end up demanding a great deal of your time and energy, and it would be easy to focus all your attention on it. It is also important to keep in mind that your customers or clients will not wait and that you have to keep the daily "business as usual" going or your business will suffer.

Plan how to balance these two equally important needs so that you do not neglect either. Look for ways in which you can manage your work flow to give you more time for your strategic leadership (building up stock, for example, to keep things going without your input for a period of time). If necessary, consider hiring extra help, such as temporary staff to deal with the day job, or look into appointing consultants who can help you manage the change.

Overcoming resistance

Despite your best attempts to prepare your team for the changes to come and help them understand why and how your strategy needs to happen, you may still encounter serious resistance to your plans. Your job is to understand why team members are resisting and to find ways to remove or overcome their resistance.

Understanding negative reactions

Change is often "logically" prepared by managers and leaders, but responded to emotionally by staff. Negative reactions to change often result from a lack of understanding of why it has to happen—the need for the change may not have been sufficiently well explained or staff may have received misinformation through gossip or leaks. Resistance can also stem from individuals asking "what's in it for me?" before thinking "why is it good for the organization?"

In many organizations, there are political forces at work. Groups of people may have different priorities and will seek their own outcome rather than the desired outcome of the organization. If you don't have power to influence these groups yourself, try to win the support of those who do.

Some of your strategic decisions may result in some people losing their jobs. It would be easy to assume that those who didn't are automatically happy. However, some argue that this is not the case and that those who survive feel uncertain or negative about the organization (some refer to this as survivor syndrome), thinking: "If they let my friend go this time, will it be me next time?" What is certain, however, is that staff will make a judgement about how the change happened and whether you behaved fairly. If they believe you did, they are more likely to continue to support you.

PROVIDE TRAINING
Offer training and coaching where appropriate, so that all individuals are confident in any new roles they have to perform.

Ways to minimize resistance to change

PROVIDE INFORMATION
Give detailed reasons for why the change needs to happen, and encourage questioning of the existing situation.

ENCOURAGE INVOLVEMENT
Where possible, involve individuals in the development of your strategy—they are more likely to accept it if they have played a part in its creation.

ENGINEER THE SITUATION
Create a "crisis" to encourage closer teamwork—in crisis, people usually stop silly arguments and work together on the main task.

WORK WITH THE GROUP
Provide facilitation where group resistance is a problem, and work individually with members of the group.

TACKLE FEAR
Provide reassurance that the future, under the new strategy, will be better than the present.

Guiding your team

Some managers think that setting the strategic direction and preparing their team for change is sufficient, but to get the best out of your team you need to provide guidance as the change progresses. Your role is to be their "coach"—to review their progress, help them to find ways to perform their new tasks better, offer encouragement, and reward success.

Reviewing progress

Telling someone how to swim and them being able to swim are different things; it isn't until they jump into the water that you and they know whether they have understood your instruction. The same is true when you implement a new strategy. Once you see individuals in action in their new roles, you can offer guidance on how they can do things better. Set aside time on a regular basis to meet with members of your team and review their progress on a one-to-one basis. Use this time to assess their performance against targets you have set and discuss any problems they are having in adjusting to their new role.

ASK YOURSELF... **AM I SUPPORTING MY STAFF IN THEIR NEW ROLES?**

- Have I been clear in helping my team understand what needs to happen to deliver the new strategy?
- Have my team confirmed that they understand their new roles?
- Have I scheduled time to monitor the team as it moves forward?
- Have I set aside time to make myself available to answer questions and to provide reassurance?
- Have I ensured that the organizational systems that are in place encourage the new behaviors necessary to implement the change, and will not drag the team back into their old ways?
- Have I devised ways in which to reward success?

Recognizing success

As part of the review progress, take time to assess and acknowledge what each individual is doing well. This is important, because it can be difficult for members of your team to know whether they have changed their behavior in the right way unless someone tells them that what they are doing is right. If a person doesn't receive these positive encouragements they may be unsure and are likely to feel unsatisfied (given their extra efforts) or may even drift back to doing things the old way. Your role as a manager is to encourage and reward every individual within your team for doing new things right. The effect of these positive words or rewards is to recognize and reinforce the desired new behaviors your new strategy requires.

A simple "well done" or "thank you" may be sufficient to boost the morale of individual team members, but you can also use more structured ways to mark success. If you measure your collective progress toward goals and targets, for example, you can then directly reward team members for achieving these milestones (either individually or collectively).

Tolerating mistakes

It is important to realize that, as people move out of their comfort zone, they may make more mistakes than usual. However, if you punish someone who has made a genuine mistake when trying to act in the new way, he or she is likely to stop trying new things. Instead you need to create an environment in which mistakes are tolerated in the early days of a new strategy. This will take courage on your behalf, as you are responsible for the actions of your staff, but it will lead to greater success, lower staff turnover, and less resistance to change in the long run.

ASK FOR FEEDBACK

Periodically ask your team members whether you are giving the support they need.

KNOW YOUR TEAM

Sometimes it is not what is said to you but what is not said that sends the most powerful message, so try to look out for any unspoken signs that a member of your team is struggling.

Monitoring progress

You have been through the process: you've analyzed yourself, the environment, and the market; you've assessed your options and planned your approach; and you've started to implement your strategic plan. You will not know the final outcome for three to five years—are you going to wait that long to see if you are on the right track?

Staying on course

Strategy is about the future, and despite your best attempts to analyze what might happen, you don't have any certainty that the future will be as you have predicted. There are likely to be changes to the environment (such as economic issues or new technology) and to the market—new competitors or products could remove your market, for example. You may also have unexpected internal issues in your organization. It is crucial, therefore, that you monitor your progress, by setting targets to be achieved and milestones that must be passed, if you are to ensure that your strategy remains on course to deliver the desired outcome.

Setting targets

When setting targets, think about where you are going, what it is going to take to get there, and when you aim to achieve your goals. If your strategic goal is to grow your position within the market by 40 percent, for example, you might set the goal of 15 percent growth each year. Alternatively, you might set an increased sales target of five percent in year one and 30 percent in the next year following the acquisition of a competitor. If your strategy is for your team to have a more central role with extended responsibilities in three years, you might set targets of hiring one new person with different skills in year one and two more staff in each of the following two years. Or, you might measure the flow of work on a monthly basis to check the increase in volume and type of work. Whatever measures you choose, they will help you to check that you are still on track.

Maintaining morale

Measuring your progress toward targets has the additional benefit of boosting staff morale. You already know that change may involve a period of uncertainty for all. Your role as a confident and

HOW TO...
MEASURE YOUR PROGRESS

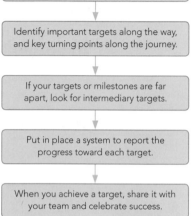

Identify the final target of your strategic plan—what are you aiming to achieve, and by when?

Identify important targets along the way, and key turning points along the journey.

If your targets or milestones are far apart, look for intermediary targets.

Put in place a system to report the progress toward each target.

When you achieve a target, share it with your team and celebrate success.

visible leader through strategic change can be enhanced by setting realistic targets and then collectively achieving them. Reaching each target can give a great sense of satisfaction to your staff and help to inspire confidence. For example, if you set an interim target for your team to decrease their processing time by 4 percent during year one and they achieve a figure of 4.5 percent, they are more likely to give that little bit extra in the following years to help you to reach your overall objective.

Managing knowledge

The implementation of a new strategy is an uncertain time—you have made changes and your team are having to deal with new challenges. Some people may decide to leave, and if they do, any knowledge they have—knowledge that could give you competitive advantage—will leave with them and be lost to your organization.

Maintaining your advantage

In some types of business, it is easy to see where knowledge is a source of competitive advantage. An accountant who has superior knowledge of taxation, for example, is best placed to save their clients money. However, important knowledge that can give a competitive advantage exists within all organizations. You may have someone who recognizes the best-quality fish on the market and buys it at the best price, or someone who has superior knowledge of donors and can attract income to a charity. As a strategic manager, it is important to look at your team and others in your organization and identify who has important knowledge, so that you can make sure that you keep it during strategic change.

IN FOCUS... TYPES OF KNOWLEDGE

Knowledge is divided into two classes: explicit or tacit. Explicit knowledge is knowledge that is easy to write down and transfer to other people: the process to be followed in producing a customer invoice, for example, or the way to assemble five components to build a product. Tacit knowledge, by comparison, is knowledge that is not easily passed on. A flute player, for example, can tell someone else how to position their fingers to make each note, but not how to bring it all together in giving a fine performance. Tacit knowledge is instinctive or learned through years of experience, and it cannot be passed on quickly or sometimes even at all.

CASE STUDY

Gaining an advantage

A consulting firm that specializes in providing advice about new environmental regulations used knowledge management to grow its business. Consulting is based on meeting the knowledge needs of clients, and the firm did this by sending an individual consultant to meet with a client and determine precisely what knowledge that client needed. The consultant would then locate the relevant knowledge through a period of research. The firm was moderately successful and built up a portfolio of clients, but was limited by the amount of time it took each consultant to work with one client. To address this, the firm put systems in place to capture the knowledge being generated by each consultant, so that it was in a form that other consultants within the firm could access. This meant that when a consultant had a similar assignment, they did not have to spend as much time researching, because they could draw upon the information that had already been gathered, saving on time and duplicated effort. In this way, the value of the knowledge was multiplied, allowing the firm to build up a larger client portfolio and increase its growth.

Capturing knowledge

As part of the implementation phase of your strategy, put in place a system to make the most of the valuable knowledge within your organization. The main function of this system is to capture important knowledge and store it in a form that you can easily access in the future. You can store it simply on paper or in files, or in electronic documents or knowledge-management software. Tailor the system you use to the importance of the information you are storing. For example, firms for which knowledge is of great advantage, such as international law firms, often invest a considerable amount of money in bespoke knowledge-management systems; smaller firms can achieve good results with word-processing and spreadsheet software.

The key to making knowledge-management systems work is cultural—you need to create an environment in which sharing knowledge is both encouraged and rewarded.

Staying on top

Strategy is not about devising and implementing a linear path toward one particular outcome—it is a way of thinking that must be in the forefront of your mind as you observe the world around you, and it must permeate every decision you make. It may take time to adopt a strategic way of thinking, but once you do it will become second nature.

Achieving success

At its heart, strategic thinking is very simple. In fact, it is as simple as one, two, three: one, where are we now? Two, where do we want to go? And three, how do we get there? It is within the role of any team leader, manager, small business owner, or organizational leader to know their current situation and what they want to achieve in the next three to five years, and to work with others to reach that goal. However, strategy is not about designing a map for the future and then setting it in stone—it is a dynamic process that defines a broad path along which you and your organization or team will achieve success.

You must always be thinking strategically. When something unexpected happens, your first thought should be "how does this affect our strategy?" and you must be ready to reevaluate or change strategy if you need to. Even once you have implemented a strategy and achieved the outcome you were hoping for, you must fight the thought that you can simply do the same again and still be successful. The world around you—the context in which you are making strategic decisions—never stays still. Stay alert to your changing environment and always look for new and better options. Strategic management is not about making continuous knee-jerk reactions to a series of unconnected events—it is about making a conscious choice to create your future.

TIP

NEVER STAND STILL
Remember that all strategies have a "shelf life"—not because they were wrong in the first place but because the world around them has changed. Make sure you have a new strategy before this happens.

CHECKLIST **MAINTAINING YOUR STRATEGIC APPROACH**

	YES	NO
• Do you list "wanting to create the future" of your team or organization amongst your chief aims?	☐	☐
• Are you continually looking for new and different ways to create sustainable competitive advantage?	☐	☐
• Do you make regular assessments of the environment you operate in, even when you are doing well?	☐	☐
• Do you always consider ways in which to match what you can do to what the world needs?	☐	☐
• Do you make sure that your strategies don't just stay on paper, but that you drive implementation through and make a difference?	☐	☐
• Do you assess every decision you make in the light of your overall strategic direction?	☐	☐

Index

Acknowledgments

Author's acknowledgments

I very much want to thank Peter Jones at DK for this opportunity. Working with the people at cobalt id has also been a delight and I should like to thank Marek for his belief and Kati for her calm and charming guidance in so many important areas.

As always, my family has shown complete support to my endeavors. To my wife Liz and my children, Rose, Dan, and Sam, thank you for everything and not least your patience over the summer holidays.

This book is dedicated to all of you who take on the role of creating the future.

Publisher's acknowledgments

The publisher would like to thank Hilary Bird for indexing, Judy Barratt for proofreading, and Chuck Wills for coordinating Americanization.

Picture credits

The publisher would like to thank the following for their kind permission to reproduce their photographs:

1 Corbis: Gregor Schuster/zefa; 4–5 Corbis: Holger Winkler/zefa; 11: Getty Images; 12–13 istockphoto.com: Jaap2; 21 Alamy: Worldspec/NASA; 27 istockphoto.com: blackred; 28–29 istockphoto.com: Chris Schmidt; 31 istockphoto.com: blackred; 32 Alamy: Tony Cortizas, Jr; 39 Getty Images: Michael Betts; 40–41: Dorling Kindersley; 43 Alamy: Russell Kord; 46 Dorling Kindersley: Kim Taylor; 48 istockphoto.com: Clint Scholz; 54 istockphoto.com: Mark Stay; 61 istockphoto.com: Selahattin Bayram; 64 istockphoto.com: Svetlana Tebenkova; 68 istockphoto.com: Roberto Caucino

Every effort has been made to trace the copyright holders. The publisher apologizes for any unintentional omission and would be pleased, in such cases, to place an acknowledgment in future editions of this book.